Lecture is Not Dead
Ten Tips for Delivering Dynamic Lectures in the College Classroom

Jennifer Patterson Lorenzetti

ISBN: 0692342230
ISBN-13: 978-0692342237

DEDICATION

This work is dedicated to the faculty of the History Department at Miami University, who taught me that lectures can be the most interesting, stimulating, and memorable part of a course.

And to my parents, Janice C. and Michael A. Patterson, who made sure I could fulfill my dream of attending this fine university.

Listen to almost any expert on higher education pedagogy, and they will tell you that the traditional lecture is dead. The "sage on the stage" has been replaced by the "guide on the side," and instructors who grew up in lecture-based classrooms must now step aside to create a multimedia extravaganza designed to hold the attention of even the most distracted of multitaskers.

Let me tell you a secret: the lecture is not dead. Yes, the world of higher education benefits greatly from the number of tools at a professor's disposal. Our classes can be much richer because we have computer technology, the internet, and perhaps our school's learning management system at our – and our students' – fingertips at all time. No one wants to take these tools away.

But the lecture has worked for centuries because, at heart, it is about human interaction, the most powerful, attention-grabbing tool for interaction at anyone's disposal. The presence of a live, active, engaged human being who is an expert in his or her field will do more to ignite the passions of a group of students than will any canned multimedia presentation.

What Dynamic Lecture is Not

Of course, not every lecture is a dynamic lecture, and it is important to distinguish a dynamic lecture from ones that will drain the life from your classroom. There are some practices that sound the death knell for any lecture, whether they be in an introductory-level college classroom or in a keynote address for a major conference. These practices are the ones that give lecture a bad name, conjuring up images of Professor Binns, the History professor from the *Harry Potter* books. Professor Binns, for those who did not read the series, was an old professor so dull that when he died, his spirit arose from his body and continued on to class, there to spend the remainder of eternity delivering the same boring lectures he had for decades. Face it, if you can make something as exciting as the Goblin Wars sound dull, you need to work on your delivery!

So how do you avoid making your students wish for an out-of-body experience of their own? Consider a few of these "commandments" that will help you avoid lecture-induced narcolepsy:

1. Thou shalt not script thy lecture.

I once took a class from a brilliant professor who, alas, had perfected his lectured down to the last example and the perfect joke – 30 years prior to the year I took the class. While the professor had all of his facts down perfectly, his insistence on scripting meant that he was delivering an oration, not teaching a class.

Scripting a talk has its place. If you are accepting a Nobel Prize or a nomination for President of the United States, you should absolutely script your remarks. You do this not because the original delivery is paramount, but because you know your audience will later look at transcripts of your address, looking for additional meaning and perhaps questioning your choice of words and phrases. In these cases, you sacrifice some spontaneity for perfection in posterity.

In a classroom, however (or in most less formal situations), scripting a lecture will drain the life from your subject. Even the most passionate lecturer will lose some of the fire and cadence that characterizes human conversation when reading prepared remarks. And it is your tone of voice as much as your content that will draw your students in.

Prepare your remarks, certainly. But restrict your cue cards or crib notes to bulleted points that you can glance at as you speak. If you are teaching a class, you already know the subject better than your students. Be confident in your knowledge and converse, rather than orate.

2. Thou shalt not read thy PowerPoint slides.

The modern cousin of scripting a lecture is reading one's comments directly off the PowerPoint slides, certainly the kiss of death for any lecture. How would you react as a student? Your professor has come to class, turned off the lights, and started reading his or her lecture directly off the slides projected at the front of the room. No wonder students fall asleep.

PowerPoint slides, or, indeed, any type of multimedia addition to your class, is a supplement to your lecture, not a summary of it. Your PowerPoint deck is a place to show visual representations or examples of content you are discussing. While you might elect to put a phrase or two on the slides, the deck should not become a substitute for your lecture. Consider a rule of thumb: if distribution of your PowerPoint deck to the class would eliminate the need for your students to take notes, you are including too much information on them.

3. Thy lectern is not a life raft.

One unintended side effect of being tied to your scripted notes or to your PowerPoint outline is that you are more likely to stake out a position in the room and hold onto it. This is particularly true for those of us who are introverts by nature – and many, many university faculty members are. Holding onto a lectern or remaining seated behind a desk in a small class feels safe and protected, and it is an easy choice.

However, it also creates "blind spots" in the classroom where certain students will have more difficulty seeing or hearing, and those will be the spots selected by students who want to tune out during class. As we will see, making yourself a "moving target" in the classroom will help to stir the energy and make sure that all students can see you and you can see all of them.

How to Create a Dynamic Lecture Environment

A dynamic lecture environment will require a fair amount of preparation on the part of the instructor, and not a small amount of improvisation. If this makes you nervous, don't worry. You will soon adapt to the demands of the dynamic lecture environment. In the meantime, begin by adopting the practices best suited to your current style, then branch out into those that are more of a stretch.

1. Bring passion to the lecture

Every dynamic lecture starts with the passion of the presenter. As college faculty, we are lucky; we automatically are asked only to lecture on subjects that we are passionate about.

Yes, I can hear the eyes roll as you contemplate that 100-level class that you'd rather not teach this year or that area of your field that you secretly dislike. But I contend that even those classes and topics are ones that you are passionate about, albeit less so than some others. You chose your field to dedicate your life to; you have that passion if you know how to tap it.

The secret, I find, is to let students hear your genuine reaction to specific parts of your course content in which you are particularly interested. Consider places in your lecture you could start a discussion with the following sentence openers:

- OK, now this is really cool....
- I read this awesome book over the summer, and it talked about this very topic....
- Now, this concept is one that I think is pretty difficult to understand, so I want us to spend some time on it...
- Here's something that I found hard to grasp the first time through...
- Did you hear the news today? Researchers at XYZ University just found....
- Now, this is worth looking up on YouTube when you have the chance...

- Someone find this out for me....

Any of these or similar openings demonstrate to your students that you continue to learn about your own field and that you continue to be excited by it. Often, students will contribute what they have seen about a relevant news item, or you will hear the sounds of the YouTube clip you referenced playing softly in the classroom. This is not distraction from your lecture; this is student engagement.

2. Let your subject matter breathe, and meet students where they are

You are an expert in your subject matter; if you weren't, you wouldn't be teaching your class. But I would contend that you have even more work to do if you can't think of at least four or five ways of getting to the point that you want to make over the course of your lecture.

In my history class, I often start by polling the class on what historical dramas or movies they have had occasion to watch: *The Great Gatsby, Titanic, Downton Abbey, Mad Men,* and the like. Not all of these are directly connected with my topic area, which is advertising history, but all of them give me a starting point that I can use to help students visualize a certain point, whether it is the sense of cultural abandon that permeated the 1920s, the rigid class structure of the British nobility, or the male-dominated workplace of the 1960s. From there, I can connect up from something the students know to something they need to learn.

I think of this as letting my lectures breathe. On my "lesson plans," which are really just loose collections of bullet points I use to cue myself about topics that support my point, I list multiple ways of making the same basic point. If I want to talk about socioeconomic stratification in the 1970s, I can talk about disco music and the movie *Saturday Night Fever,* or I can talk about London-based punk rock and the migration to CBGB's in New York. I will start with the cultural touchstone most familiar to my students (which varies from year to year) and I will eventually work my way to my main point.

3. Log some miles

If holding onto your lectern is the kiss of death, then it follows that you are going to have to let that life raft go and start moving around. Make sure that your lavaliere microphone is wireless, get a pair of comfortable shoes (I have a pair of 3" heeled sandals with cork soles for this very purpose) and prepare to start walking up and down the classroom rows. Buy yourself a pedometer if you need the incentive, and see how many of your daily 10,000 steps you can log during a single Chem 101 class.

Obviously, your degree of freedom will be dictated somewhat by the size of your classroom. If you are teaching a class of several hundred in an auditorium, you may be restricted to walking back and forth across the stage; if you are in a smaller room, there is no reason why you can't walk up and down rows and land in the back, the front, or on the side of the room.

Moving around like this has several benefits. First, students are much less likely to sleep, text, surf the web, or engage in other non-class behaviors if you are likely to wind up standing behind them. Although you may never get rid of distracted behaviors by all students, you will teach them that they need to be able to click back to a notes page and appear awake at any time, because they don't know when you might show up.

Second, you give everyone in the room a chance to see and hear you, which is critical when giving a dynamic lecture. Your facial expressions, your gestures, and the way you interact with the class are all critical to conveying your information, and you give everyone an equal chance to be recognized and heard by you and to be exposed to your inflection and your behavior up close.

I recommend doing more than walking, in fact. In my classes, I pace off the size of a tape drive on an original WWII-era computer, I gesture to indicate how my posture would change if I were wearing an S-bend corset, and I even lead my class in an impromptu Charleston lesson that migrates into a basic salsa step they can use at their next weekend outing. There is a decent chance that my students are laughing at me when they leave the room, but there's also a decent chance that they remember my antics after class is adjourned for the summer.

4. The internet is our friend.

One of the most difficult things for me to get used to when I was a new instructor was the presence of the internet in the classroom. When I was in college, professors would ask for questions at the end of class, then carefully note any they could not answer. They would research these questions as needed and answer them at the beginning of the next class.

My, how things change. No more quickly can I say "I'm not sure," then I have a student who has harnessed the power of Google to find an answer. I have learned to love this about my classes. Students who want to prove that they can answer a question I can't prove to me that they are listening and using critical thinking skills to engage with my lecture. I try to stop and ask about the source that they have found for their information, and, if necessary, the class takes a detour into assessing the reliability of internet sources. I always follow up in a class-wide email that I send after every class meeting, verifying the information and giving a link to the correct answer to the question.

5. Use the whiteboard as a supplement, not a note-taking proxy

The old saying about writing on a board is "chalk and talk." We may have updated things to favor white boards and markers over blackboards and talk, but the concept remains the same: your writing should supplement your conversation, not replace it.

Remember that all of your actions during a lecture should create a learning experience for your students. If you go overboard with whiteboard notes, your students will only record what you write and ignore or minimize what your say.

On the other hand, if you write too little, you risk students being confused about what you have said and what terms you think are important. Then, students' attention will be divided, but it will be by a frustrating search for new and unfamiliar terms.

Your lecture should create an opportunity for auditory, kinesthetic, and visual learning: Auditory, of course, comes from the sound of your lecture. Kinesthetic comes from the experience of writing or typing notes (and there is evidence to suggest that students remember what they hand wrote better then what they type). Finally, the visual component comes both from what you write on the board and from what your students put down in notes. It is a powerful combination.

So what sorts of things should you write on the board? A partial list might be:

- Steps of a problem or equation as you solve it

- Rough schematics or maps

- Diagrammed sentences

- New terms from your discipline the students may not know

- Any vocabulary words that generate looks of confusion

- Brainstormed lists, especially when you are helping students sort valuable ideas from wild guesses contributed by their peers

- Markers or signposts for the lecture, such as topic headings or dates

6. PowerPoint is a supplement, not a summary

Everything you have heard about giving great speeches applies to giving great lectures, and this includes avoiding what is rightly called "death by PowerPoint."

If you choose to use a projected slide deck during your lectures, do so on a limited basis. In no case should you draft your entire class lecture on PowerPoint and then project it as you read along. Your students will have little incentive to attend class and stay alert and engaged if they know they will be sitting for an hour in darkness listening to you read. Not only is this mind-numbing for the students, but they will invariably -- and wisely -- ask you to email out your PowerPoint deck. In one motion, you will have eliminated the note-taking part of the experience that is so valuable in helping students remember the material. You will also be tempted to stick close to your slide text, so the spontaneity that comes from allowing students to ask questions and make comments that take your lecture in new directions is diminished.

This is not to say that there is no place for a PowerPoint deck in your presentation. I like to use short slide decks to show supplemental material, like cultural artifacts. In my History of Advertising class, I prepare a deck for each unit of the course that shows certain cultural materials like photos of events or illustrations of period fashion, and then I include slides of advertising from the period with no text on the slide other than a citation for the piece. The advertisements become the basis for discussion as I ask students to contribute their assessment of advertising techniques used, color choices, font choices, core messaging, and other elements. Obviously, even if I elect to share the deck with students after class, it would be relatively useless as a study tool without attendance in the class and careful notes on the discussion.

7. Add multimedia elements with a twist

If you keep up with pedagogical fads, you know that many currently believe that today's students, especially of the Millennial generation (born 1981-2001) cannot learn without multimedia elements. But often, these thinkers disregard the true breadth of the term "multimedia" and use it to mean only computer-based elements, especially video.

Video is wonderful, but not all video is created equal. If you've selected a multimedia element for your class that is simply a recording of a talking head, look further. If all you've accomplished with your video element is letting another person take over the lecture, you would be much further ahead bringing in a guest speaker who can take questions.

Instead, remember that all multimedia elements you use in class should support your conversation with your students you are having via your lecture, and your elements don't have to have a cord or a URL to be valuable. In my class, I bring a certain number of historical artifacts, including primary source books and articles to pass around, and even elements of my own outfit of the day that reflect something important about the period under consideration I can refer to. Although I do use a certain number of YouTube videos and web sites, I generally prefer to share these items in an email I send to the class after each lecture period. They can view or explore these elements on their own time in preparation for the next class.

8. Say everything important two (or more) different ways

Some instructors seem to view a lecture class as a game of hide and seek. The important facts and ideas that will appear on the test are hidden, mentioned only once in the lecture or buried somewhere in the supplemental readings. They seem to believe that the purpose of a class is to encourage students to go over materials with a fine toothed comb, looking for those facts that might translate to points on the exam.

While you might terrorize some particularly diligent students into playing this game, I think the real purpose of a lecture class is to explore, elucidate, and make perfectly clear all of the important points that you would like students to remember. I try to always mention every important concept at least twice: once in a large, all-class discussion of the concept, and once again in a peripheral way as review.

For example, when I discuss the growth of the post-WWII suburbs, I ask my students to imagine how women who formerly held defense jobs during the war might have felt when they achieved the goal of having their sweethearts home to start a family in a tract house with all of the modern luxuries. We list ideas on the board: some felt relieved, some were happy to not have to work, some were excited to move on into being a wife and mother. But what about those women – many of them, at the time – who were left at home without transportation because most families had only one car? What role did loneliness play in their lives? How stimulating was keeping the kitchen floor at a high shine compared to assembling bombs to help win an epic war? What was it like to suddenly be dependent on a husband for spending money? All of these ideas come up again when we discuss the home-centered advertising of the period and then again when we discuss the feminism of the 1960s. Of course, these concepts are also available in their class readings, and I email supplemental materials to highlight the concept after class is over. Ideally, my students are not surprised to see an essay question asking them to discuss the demographic trend of the stay-at-home housewife of the late 1940s and 1950s.

One of the reasons often given for a switch to multimedia-heavy classes is the desire to provide content that works well for all learning styles, broadly grouped into visual, auditory, and kinesthetic. Your lecture-based class can provide these opportunities as well:

- Visual learners will benefit from the use of slides, white board notes and drawings, and artifacts that you bring to class. Also, if you encourage note-taking, their notes will be a visual record of the material.
- Similarly, auditory learners are receiving information in their preferred learning modality as you speak. Encourage these students and their classmates to speak as well, adding to the discussion.
- Kinesthetic learners are often a challenge, because so much of a lecture class involves sitting still. Encourage these students to take notes by hand, rather than using a computer. Some research suggests that the process of writing by hand makes a greater impression on someone's memory, and my own experience bears this out. I think lecture is a great opportunity to use the note-taking process to turn auditory input into a kinesthetic event that creates a visual product.

Think about ways you can incorporate different components into a class. If you are a chemistry prof lecturing about a certain molecular structure, you can always pass around a physical model while you speak. Visual learners will have something extra to look at, and kinesthetic learners will have something to feel and interact with. Try to make all of your important points with an eye to multiple learning modalities.

9. Tell stories.

I once had a colleague tell me, "the students just want to hear stories." I had to agree. Most people, whether they are young or old, in school or not, want to hear a good story.

Think about the way human beings have always learned and remembered their history and lore. Pre-literate societies depended on story-tellers who were part of the tribe or who journeyed from town to town, telling, chanting, and singing stories that would be repeated over and over. Some of our most enduring literature started out as a story to be told – *Beowulf* is just one example.

Many classroom lectures become dry because we strip the story of the facts and leave the bare bones of the subject for our students. I encourage you to put the story back in your lecture. If your subject involves human beings (and most do), make sure you are telling stories with protagonists, antagonists, challenges, triumphs, heroes, and villains. Ask students what they expect will happen next. Then, hold them to some real sophisticated analysis – what do their critical thinking skills lead them to predict will happen? How do they know? In the example above in which my class discusses the post-WWII housewife, I buttress my story with class discussion about what sorts of advertising messages would appeal most to these women. I expect the class to be able to differentiate among advertising techniques we have studied to pick the ones that will be most effective, but I depend on the story to make the situation something they will remember.

10. Encourage your students to pick the low-hanging fruit.

Finally, encourage class participation in your lecture class. Just because the teaching method is "lecture," you don't have to be the only one to speak. Encourage students to shout out theories and answers, weigh in on questions, and give an opinion.

I often tell my students, "don't be afraid to pick the low-hanging fruit." As I move into a topic that I want them to discuss critically, I will often start with a basic fact question, or a question that has its own answer embedded in it. ("Do you think employment rates at the beginning of the Great Depression were increasing or decreasing?") This has two purposes. First, it breaks the ice by getting a student to contribute to the discussion by answering a question with a high probability of choosing a correct answer. Second, it allows the students to start remembering important issues they will use in future critical analysis. In the example given, we talk frequently about the impact that an economic downturn will have on the advertising for various products. I want the students to remember in the future that plummeting employment correlates with an economic downturn, so this is one opportunity for them to practice identifying this circumstance.

Preparing the Dynamic Lecture: A Checklist

- Think about your lecture topic for the day. On a separate sheet of paper, list the major points that all students should walk away with.

- Consider the levels of information you want the students to learn. Do you want them to remember discrete facts? Add facts up to reach a conclusion? Defend a position based on the information?

- Decide on at least one anecdote, story, or interesting fact that you can use to illustrate each point.

- Decide how you will convey each of these points visually. Do you have a photo in your PowerPoint deck for the day? Will you draw a map on the white board? List important vocabulary as you speak? Act out a concept?

- Decide which of your points can be reflected kinesthetically. Can you bring in a physical item to pass around the room? Is there an exercise that would get students out of their seats, however briefly, to illustrate the point?

- Start your class with a quick review of the previous class. Ask students to help you "recap the story" to that point.

- Inform the students of the broad outline of topics you plan to cover that day. Consider putting a brief checklist on the board so students can organize their notes and understand the pacing of your lecture.

- After your lecture, give a brief recap of what was covered and a quick overview of what will happen in the next class.

- Consider sending an all-class email shortly after your class session with supplemental materials, answers to questions, and fun facts about the topics at hand.

Discussion Guide

If you are using this book as part of a faculty development session, consider discussing these questions as part of your session.

1. How would you describe your class format?

2. Do you consider yourself a lecturer? Why or why not?

3. What sort of room do you typically teach in – size, seating configuration, A/V set-up? What challenges does this pose for your lecture?

4. How many students do you typically teach?

5. Have you seen students lose interest or "zone out" during lecture? What are you doing when this happens?

6. What concepts from your class do students find hardest to grasp?

7. What concepts or skills are the most important for students to learn? You might want to consult your course objectives.

8. How can you convey these concepts or develop these skills by using stories? Descriptions? Visual aids? Supplementary out-of-class videos? Kinesthetic experiences?

9. What do you find most challenging or anxiety-producing about lecturing?

10. What do you like the best or think you do the best?

ABOUT THE AUTHOR

Hi! I'm Jennifer Patterson Lorenzetti, and I'm the owner of Hilltop Communications.

I'm an experienced independent writer specializing in science and medical writing, market research and analysis, industry reports, business and technology coverage, K-12 and higher education coverage, and corporate communications. I am a confident public speaker and educator focusing on academic and training audiences and topics, and I'm available to consult with institutions of higher education on marketing communications materials, faculty/staff development, and building academic programs.

I founded Hilltop Communications in 1997, and it has quickly grown to serve clients in many different industries with a variety of challenging projects ranging from journalistic coverage for trade magazines to analysis for industry and marketing research reports to copywriting for corporate communications and advertising. I also deliver webinars and provide customized speaking and training for a variety of organizations.

Prior to founding Hilltop Communications, I earned a Master's degree in higher education administration from Miami University and worked for a number of universities as registrar, academic advisor, and in admission, financial aid, and alumni affairs. Since the founding of Hilltop Communications, I have also become an adjunct professor (history is a favorite subject) and have served as Academic Dean for a small privately-held college.

In my spare time, my husband and I enjoy ballroom and salsa dancing and are avid gardeners. We also share a love of Key West, Florida, and try to visit whenever possible.

www.ingramcontent.com/pod-product-compliance
Lightning Source LLC
Chambersburg PA
CBHW060551030426
42337CB00021B/4530